Rasheed's Family Goes for a Ride

Mini Mu'min Du'a Series #10

www.Mini-Mumin.com

Copyright © 2012 Mini Mu'min Publications

All rights reserved. This publication may not be reproduced in whole or in part by any means whatsoever without written permission from the copyright owner.

Introduction

All praise is due to Allah the Most High, may Allah send His blessings on the Prophet Muhammad (saw), his family, his companions, and those who follow him in righteousness until the Day of Judgment.

"And remember your Lord by your tongue and within yourself, humbly and in awe, without loudness, by words in the morning and the afternoon, and be not among those who are neglectful." (Holy Qur'an 7:205)

The **Mini Mu'min Du'a Series** is designed to help you teach your child essential Islamic supplications and the situations in which they would be used. Each book focuses on a single topic, with key vocabulary **highlighted**. These key words can then serve as a tool to remind your child of important points. All supplications are shown in Arabic text, translation, and transliteration. For any assertions regarding fiqh we have provided textual proofs, from the Qur'an and authentic Sunnah of the Prophet (saw), at the bottom of the relevant page. Each story is accompanied by original artwork, but in accordance with Islamic beliefs we do not use human or animal images.

Transliteration has been provided here as a means to help those who do not know Arabic to teach supplications to their children. But it must be noted that all transliteration is imperfect and cannot accurately represent Arabic sounds in their entirety. We therefore encourage anyone who uses our books to use the transliteration as a tool, but not an end in itself, and to eventually learn the supplications in the original Arabic.

In some cases, sounds will be represented in the transliteration (because they are present in the Arabic text) that will not actually be pronounced. These generally occur at the end of a supplication and are related to the Arabic rules for pausing and stopping. To clarify this for non-Arabic speakers, we have placed brackets [ ] around those sounds in the transliteration that would not be pronounced when reciting the supplication.

Thank you for purchasing this book, may Allah benefit both you and your child through it, forgive us for any errors we have made, and benefit us in this life and the Hereafter if there is any good in it.

That (He) has created pairs in all things, and has made for you ships and cattle on which you ride. In order that you may sit firm and square on their backs, and when so seated, you may celebrate the (kind) favor of your Lord, and say:

'Glory is to Him Who has provided this (transport) for us though we could never have had it by our own efforts. Surely unto our Lord we are returning.'

(Holy Qur'an 43:12-14)

The sun was shining warmly,
Gentle breezes stirred the air,

The grass was green as green could be,
Flowers bloomed brightly everywhere!

Birds in their nests chirped cheerfully,
The bees in their hives were all abuzz…

And everyone at Rasheed's house
Was happy and excited, too
BECAUSE….

They were getting ready to take a ride,
Since it was such a beautiful day!

Stopping at a special spot they knew,
To have a picnic along the way.

Rasheed always enjoyed a good picnic,
But the ride was his favorite part.

So many things to see along the way,
He could hardly wait to start!

A tin of oatmeal raisin cookies,
Soft and chewy, was already packed.

A big bowl of potato salad was ready,
And delicious sandwiches were stacked.

A thermos filled with sweet iced tea,
And a blanket folded nice and neat,

Everything was all set to go,
The picnic preparations were complete!

Rasheed's father was loading the car,
And his mother was checking her list,

Making sure they had everything,
And that nothing would be missed.

Rasheed was helping his little sister,
So, he opened the car door wide-

"When we get into a car," he asked,
"Why don't we just jump inside?"

"We have to make du'a,[1]" Hajar said,
Holding Rasheed's hand very tight.

"You know what?" he said smiling,
"You are absolutely right!"

So, they made the **Du'a for Riding**,[2]
It's the way each ride should begin…

They started by remembering Allah,
Saying "**Bismillaah**" as they stepped in.

---

[1] The du'a made when riding in a vehicle or on an animal (i.e. any form of transport).

[2] See footnote #6

Next, they said, "**Alhamdu lillah**,"
As they each **sat down**[3] in their seat.

But wait, they were not quite done,
Their du'a was not yet complete…

Then, they **thanked Allah**
For the **blessing** of having a **car**,

Because without the things we ride in
We wouldn't be able to go very far!

---
[3] See footnote #6

Du'a for Riding in a Vehicle

سُبْحَانَ الَّذِي سَخَّرَ لَنَا هَذَا وَ مَا كُنَّا لَهُ مُقْرِنِينَ وَ إِنَّا إِلَى رَبِّنَا لَمُنْقَلِبُونَ، الْحَمْدُ لِلَّهِ، الْحَمْدُ لِلَّهِ، الْحَمْدُ لِلَّهِ، اللَّهُ أَكْبَرُ، اللَّهُ أَكْبَرُ، اللَّهُ أَكْبَرُ، سُبْحَانَكَ اللَّهُمَّ إِنِّي ظَلَمْتُ نَفْسِي فَاغْفِرْ لِي، فَإِنَّهُ لاَ يَغْفِرُ الذُّنُوبَ إِلاَّ أَنْتَ.

"Subhaanal-lathee sakhkhara lanaa haatha wa maa kunnaa lahu muqrineen. Wa innaa ilaa Rabbinaa lamunqaliboon. Alhamdu lillaah, alhamdu lillaah, alhamdu lillaah, Allaahu Akbar, Allaahu Akbar, Allaahu Akbar, subhaanakal-laahumma innee dhalamtu nafsee faghfir lee, fa innahu laa yaghfiruth-thunooba illa Ant[a]."

(Glory is to Him Who has provided this [transport] for us though we could never have had it by our own efforts. Surely unto our Lord we are returning. Praise is to Allah, Praise is to Allah, Praise is to Allah, Allah is the Greatest, Allah is the Greatest, Allah is the Greatest. Glory is to You, Oh Allah, I have wronged my own soul. Forgive me, for surely none forgives sins but You.)

Then, Rasheed and Hajar **laughed**,[4]
When their du'a was all done,

Because **Allah was pleased** with them,
And how they had begun.

Now, they were REALLY ready,
Ready to go for a ride!

Because they had remembered,
To make du'a as they got inside.

---
[4] See footnote #6

Rasheed **buckled**[5] himself and Hajar in,
As their parents got in the car, too.

Hajar declared quite cheerfully,
"We made our **du'a**,[6] did you?"

"Of course," said her mother laughing,
As her father smiled and started the car,

"We always have to **remember Allah**
When **riding** anywhere- near or far."

---

[5] Always remember safety when riding in a vehicle, buckle up.

[6] 'Ali ibn Rabi'ah said: I saw 'Ali ibn Abi Talib (ra) when he brought an animal to mount and when placing his foot in the stirrup, saying: *In the name of Allah*, and when he had seated himself on its back he said: *Praise be to Allah*. Then he said: *Gloried be He who has subdued these for us, and we were not capable of doing so; and verily to our Lord we are returning.* Then he said: *Praise be to Allah*- three times. Then he said: *Allah is the Greatest*- three times. Then he said: *How far are You from every imperfection! O Allah, I have acted wrongly against myself, so forgive me, for there is no one who forgives sins but You.* Then he gave a laugh, and (someone) said: O Commander of the Faithful, what did you laugh for? He said: I saw the Prophet (saw) do as I have done, then he gave a laugh, and I said: O Messenger of Allah, what did you laugh for? He said, "Your Lord is pleased at His servant when he says: *O Lord, forgive my sins*- knowing that no one forgives sins but I." (Abu Dawud 14/2602, and Al-Albaani graded it as "Sahih" in his *Sahih Sunan Abi Dawud* 14/2602. See also: *Sahih Kalimat-Tayyib* #138 pg. 66)

They backed out of their driveway,
Starting down their little street.

Rasheed and Hajar looked out,
At all the houses lined up nice and neat.

Painted all kinds of different colors,
Some made of brick and others wood,

Each family tried to make their house,
As cozy as they could!

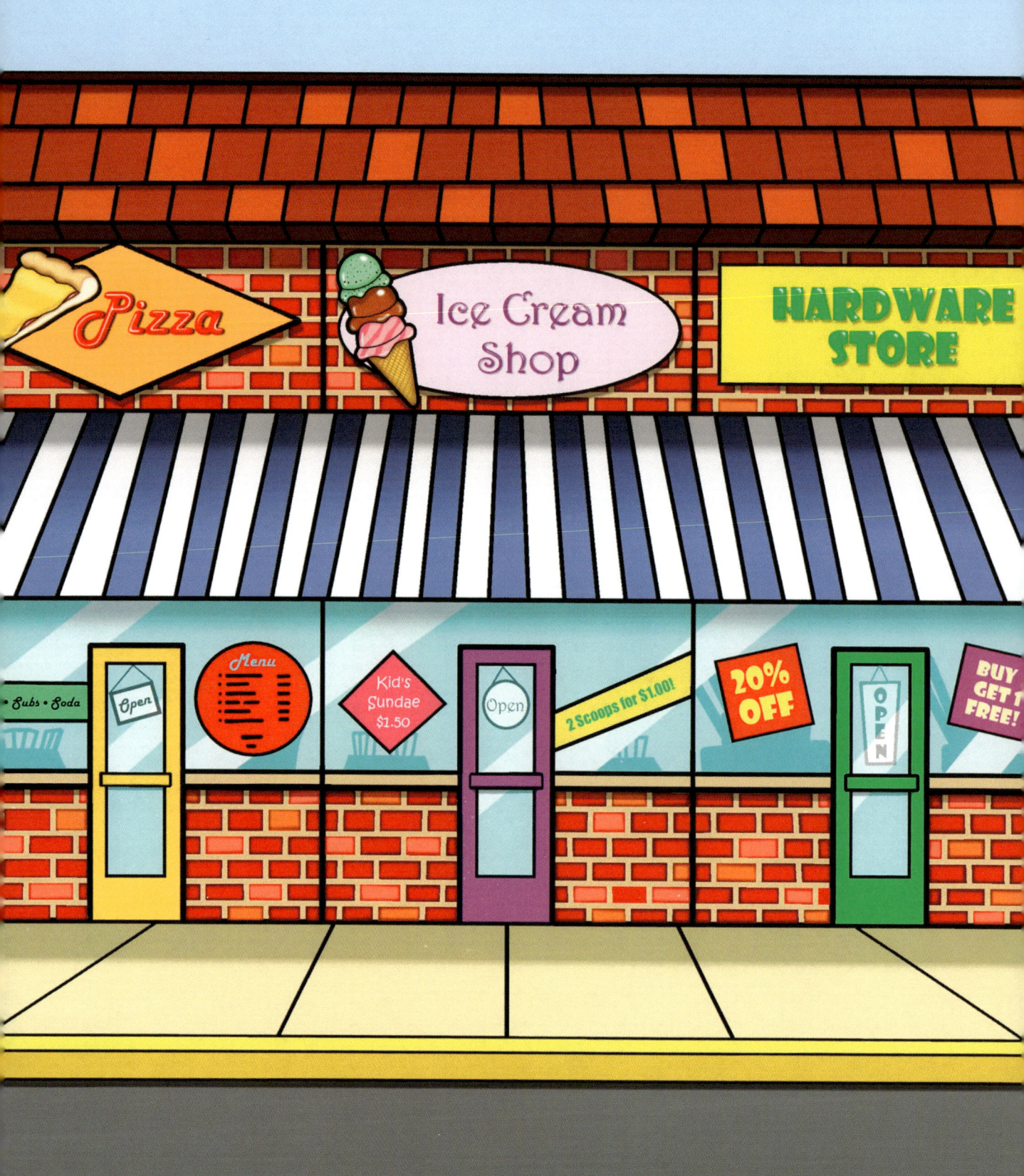

As they left their neighborhood,
They came into the big Town Square.

They saw the Masjid where they went,
For Jummah[7] and for daily prayer.

Then, they turned onto Main Street-
It had lots of interesting stores!

Signs of every shape and color hung
In the windows and on the doors.

---

[7] "Jummah" -The Friday Prayer

They rode past the big red Firehouse,
The Post Office, and the Halal Mart.

The buildings started to spread out,
Growing farther and farther apart.

As they came to the edge of town,
The land became open and wide,

Green grassy fields and barns replaced
The houses and stores on each side.

Suddenly, they bounced up and down-
Their wheel had hit a rock in the road!

Just like when an animal **trips**[8]
When carrying a heavy load.

They didn't get upset, say bad things,
Or waste their time with grumbling…

Instead they all said,[9]

> بِسْمِ اللَّهِ
>
> *"Bismillaah"*
> (In the name of Allah)

The **du'a** when your ride is **stumbling**.

---

[8] The du'a made when the mounted animal (or means of transport) stumbles.

[9] Narrated Abul Malih (ra), on the authority of a man: I was riding on a mount behind the Prophet (saw) when his mount stumbled. I said: May the devil parish! He said, "Do not say: 'May the devil perish!' for if you say that, he will swell so much that he will be like a house, and say: 'By my power'. But say: '*In the name of Allah*'; for when you say that, he will diminish so much so that he will be like a fly." (Abu Dawud 41/4946, and Al-Albaani graded it as "Sahih" in his *Sahih Sunan Abi Dawud* 2/4982. See also: *Sahih Kalimat-Tayyib* #184 pg. 81)

Up ahead the road began to rise,
Soon they could see for miles around.

You feel so much bigger up high,
Than when you are on lower ground.

So, they all said,[10]

> اللَّهُ أَكْبَرُ
>
> "Allaahu Akbar"
> (Allah is the Greatest)

As they reached the **top of the hill**,

Because no matter how high you go,
Remember that **Allah is Greater**[11] still.

---

[10] The du'a made while ascending during a journey.

[11] Narrated Jabir bin 'Abdullah Al-Ansari (ra): Whenever we went up a place we would say, '*Allah is the Greatest*', and whenever we went down a place we would say, '*Glory is to Allah*' (Al-Bukhaari 52/236. See also: *Sahih Kalimat-Tayyib* #140 pg. 67)

Now that they had reached the top,
They rumbled down the other side-

Rasheed and Hajar loved going fast,
It felt like a roller coaster ride!

Still, they remembered to make du'a,[12]
It's a very handy thing to know,

سُبْحَانَ اللَّهِ

"Subhaan Allaah"
(Glory is to Allah)

...is what we say,
When we ride from **high to low**![13]

---

[12] The du'a made when descending during a journey.

[13] See footnote #11

At last, they reached their special spot,
With green grass under a shady tree.

They laid out all their picnic things,
It was peaceful as could be!

The iced tea was cool and refreshing,
The sandwiches were a great start,

The potato salad was perfect,
But the cookies were the best part!

Remember, no matter where you go,
No matter how far away you roam-

All journeys must come to an end,
And then you have to go back home!

When you make the **Du'a for Riding**,
There's something important to learn-

Wherever your journey takes you,
It is to **Allah** that you will **return**![14]

---
[14] See footnote #6

The End!

Other available titles in the Mini Mu'min Du'a Series:

Batool's Bedtime Story
Bilal's Bakery
Fatimah's First Fasting Day
Jameelah Gets Dressed
Muhammed Goes to the Masjid
Saliha Sneezes
Waheeda the Wudoo' Wonder
Waleed Wakes Up

and many more!...

Visit our online bookstore at:

www.Mini-Mumin.com

Made in the USA
Charleston, SC
13 January 2014